Christine Redman-Waldeyer

Frame by Frame

Muse-Pie Press
PASSAIC, NJ
2007

Cover Art: Edgar Degas "Dancer Fastening her Pump"

R.G. Rader, editor & publisher
Muse-Pie Press
73 Pennington Avenue
Passaic, New Jersey 07055 USA

Redman-Waldeyer, Christine
Frame by Frame/Christine Redman Waldeyer
Poems.

ISBN 978 0 918453 19 8
I. Title

Frame by Frame

Contents

Acknowledgments

The following poems have been published previously:

"Pearls," "Belfast Letters (1980)," "Reflection," "Moonrise," "Despair (For Allen and Debby Murphy)," "Between Two Pictures," "Easel," " Diet," "Red Ribbon," "In the Mirror Mother" in *The Poet's Easter: A Healing of Mind, Body, and Spirit* (doctoral dissertation-2006)

"Answers," "Birds At My Window," "Finding Time," "Monarch," "Paean," "Hour Glass" (as "Rare Moments"), "Supermarket" at *Boloji*

"Easel" in *Idiom*

"Flood," "Gardner," "Wanting to Land," "One Hit Please," are forthcoming in *The Paterson Literary Review* #37 2008

Frame by Frame

Auk

called to the ocean
with bread
in hand

I'm there
and now here
with the angels
above me

tossing up
broken crumbs
to the air

Dames' Ball

Quiet and shy
I wouldn't be going to the school dance -
the dames' ball,
the one where the girls ask and pay.

No male friends,
simply I would stay at home and be shamed.
Kim, a junior, thin, athletic -
in her tom boyish beauty wouldn't have it.

By the end of that day,
the last day to buy tickets,
she had four willing dishes for me to choose.
Teddie, a senior was prime choice.

What is he like now? I asked.
My memories of him were from years ago,
fixed on the image of his fussy mother
ushering the crying, overweight Teddie into church.

They had been the only children
I came in touch with
whose parents were divorced,
foreign in that time, that place.

He's thin now and a SENIOR, not a geek, she said.
A decent pick, a senior, a counter balance
to his average boy looks and gapped tooth smile
coming now from a thinner face.

By March, my birthday, we were an item.
After his candlelit lobster dinner steamed in the trailer
behind his father's house he attempted
to give me his present by shelling out my virgin body.

If I'm going too fast, just stop me, he announced.
And soon I was mumbling
I don't want to get pregnant and want to go home.
I go home.

He kept pushing months later, sought me out now
as his graduation present. I knew it would never be him,
not my first, that crying, red-faced fat kid.
He knew it as well.

After graduation we had one more date
where at the box office he claimed
he left his wallet home.
I knew I'd never see that money,

the boy who never walked me to the door,
pushed me out of a rolling truck, never phoned.
My father called it;
our paths never crossed again.

Wired

The car rides were the most painful,
surreal in their way
as we journeyed to Carrier

It seemed so far, the ride then -
though it might have only been an hour.
Now I'm older and that much time in a car
is Everyday

Maybe it wasn't the longness of the ride
but the longness of the strange conversation
my young ears weren't ready to hear, my young
heart though willing itself to understand

"Shock treatments" was what my Papa got
at this hospital

What did that mean?

I would imagine wires and electric volts
running over him, taped to him - like Frankenstein

What hospital does such things?

He'd come out in slippers and a bathrobe, he'd kiss us
Hello in that same formality, in a family way but distant

I remember large windows from large rooms
and green tight lawns, stretching its green over
land like it was a skin -
I remember they said he worried about shaving
as if the worry was a stranger in his mind pacing

Then again what does one worry about when they can
And I think of vacations where I forgot my razor -
Where showers can't erase the growing stubble from my
legs clean

but I never really remembered the ride home
He wasn't there once, or even just twice
I remember they said at first
it was because my grandma died,

The lady who stayed upstairs in bed
when we'd visit, who would knit my cat cat doll clothes -
I couldn't see her but they sent down tiny sweaters, little
smocks,
and small hats

I guess after her stomach swelled
the cancer ate the rest of her,
I try but can't remember her voice, or smell

I guess he did -
that was why he was there -
My Uncle and Mom, his sister Jean
I'd hear them talk and whatever he had

my Uncle must of caught

And he fell too - from that branch of Life
that breaks when the weight on it gets too heavy

It's not all I remember -
I remember how he, my Papa, could still
do headstands - I was proud
He surely wasn't like most grandfathers

And in the basement too, there was that drawing
His self-portrait and he's sailing on a boat
Another self-portrait, he was self-made - didn't need

that college education, made it with his mind and hands -
That was why they lived by the lake where the rich go
I loved that house, the many long halls and mirrors

I wanted to draw like him
and be slim enough when
I was old to turn upside down.

Pumpkin Spells

The knife pushes into the line
I've drawn around its top
and I penetrate the circle,
wiggle the hat off, scoop the insides out.

Slips of torn paper hold their names
and I drop them in one by one
The potion has begun once I've added
a bit of honey, sugar -

a pinch of brown and white.
A tablespoon of molasses is whisked in
before I wet it with sacred water and rum
The wooden spoon stirs it to a paste

before I cap it.
Two white candles nearby are howling
and tails are wagging in circles
Sour grapes on the vine turn ripe

In this daydream,
I nearly forget the Latino girl
who stands before me, still a stranger
in my classroom

Her shirt hangs softly off her shoulder
and running mascara spills onto
the crumbled papers she holds for me to see
The man she loves beat her,

those bruises on display.
I dream of driving pumpkins
through the large gold hoops of her earrings,
those pumpkins that dared us

with Cinderella to believe in fairy godmothers
who turn squash into stagecoaches
and mice into men
who open doors in tailcoats.

I wished to hold her in my arms
and tell her there aren't such things,
but the arms retreat to mark my book -
Excused Absence.

Pearls

Bought in a faraway land
when I was still young
still beautiful to imagine a day

I would wear them.

Weddings and christenings waited
for their cap and gown from life.

Funerals I had not thought of.

Theirs I had not
thought of.

Clasp brilliant in diamonds, I felt like
a movie star; A movie star without a life. Nothing
but fame and mystique.

Did I tell you those pearls I never wore? The ones
from Majorca. I didn't marry him. I married
the boy next store.

I brought them home, this treasure from over those
unknown seas. I found her number and then hers and
then hers. I finally dialed his.

I never got through. Back then, you didn't have call
waiting. Busy was his line. Busy.

I was marked to carry the pearls, not wear them. Wife
I'm not. Movie star I'm neither.

The pearls were too heavy. The earrings though in kissed
colors I have worn; studs of blue, gray, and white.

The ring I lent to another bride.

Belfast Letters (1980)

Kelley Sally, I knew you that summer,
You stayed with the Mc Enery's,
My best friend's family.

We played tag
And Barbie dolls
Under a humid New Jersey sun that August-

My summers, because of my city friends,
Reinvented my own town;
I saw nature unwrap itself under their eyes

And the sound of Bronx
Netted my curiosity of places
Where children lived in apartment buildings.

And then you came,
And I was dazzled by your voice
That sang when you spoke.

Red hair and freckles,
I envied your straight shiny hair
Against my wavy dull brown.

When you left, we promised to write and we did.
Your letters are kept in a tin box
And tell of things only a ten-year old knows

Then all I could not understand
Festered, my letters went...
But no longer did letters come in.

I cried…because I thought you had forgotten me
But my Mom told me it was because of war.
Something about Belfast

And letters lost.

Cameo

She is white, touched by yellow on her dress,
raised away from the pink of conch and beautiful,

her portrait octagon framed and in white gold
Inherited - romantic overtures dance

on my ears and heart with history;
Papa Joe always gave her the best

And I'm at the jeweler romancing myself with research,
1930's - 1940's, she says as she turns it over

Rope chain; she asks, if I'll take it in silver
Though it's cheaper and looks the same,

I can't stop my need to know
and empty pockets without hesitation because

I can put it on a card
And it radiates close around my neck, sixteen inches

Farther away, I hear the loud whispers
tell me I have inherited this *"again"*

but I cannot decipher this poetry until
Bo Derek faces me televising louder still

reminding me of ivory and tortoise shell
and our need to answer our children

as we deplete our planet
The gems from my sock drawer take on new meaning -

ivory cut earrings, clip ons
rare and also calling

Can't I adjust them to my pierced ears?
The jewelry I understand is heavier

and I am dared to look
away from romance.

Attic Treasures

Fall cleaning and I organize, toss away
all those busy, busy papers, all those
trinkets, yet somewhere,

somewhere deep, ticket stubs and
thank you cards, love letters and beads, old
pocketbooks with forgotten cash,

all my towers, all my towers built of stash
become my attic treasures as
I exchange box for box, send up

grandma's yellow bride and groom, (along with,
on top of) frames, a dish of things, and my sister's
vase from pottery class

and above me, in this chain, train to move
from closet to a land of desert and artic,
a land where the mice creep and sleep

comes lighting down,
this box of things,
until crash!

I could not weep but knew I should,
and mumbled something right,
rite of passage but not right of mind

The bride, the groom were shattered fast
and something stirred,
something of a nest to laugh, to laugh

at…

ashes that I swept back together in my task
as if the bride, the groom could glue together, so there,
there in the land above is a box of, a box of trash.

Monarch

Sweeter yellows than the sun's rays that day
Netted my heart,
As I found you torn and bedded to the ground.

Forced to trust, I guided you to my hand
A closer vision of that transition from beast to
Beauty I held now with a frown.

My children wished your wings would grow
And swell as I placed you in the flats of marigolds,
A grave itself with ending summer, an overture to brown

I knew it was near, the dust of you undone
To the brightest Orange I left you
Under shade and mourning
A King of skies, a King of transient ends…

Reflection

Before ballet class,
I bit into a firm red apple,
left one supple piece
edged in the back of my mouth

Madame...
Famed in Russia
pushed my stomach in,
straightened my back

kicked my feet into proper position
with her black street shoes,
that matched the black scarf
wound around her head.

In pictures,
she was tall and grand,
her spirit narrowed with her failing body
stern and gray as her everyday dress.

I avoided her eyes,
stared at my reflection at the bar
and gnawed secretly
at the apple through class.

Ballerina

Madame Swaboda,
Her cane, metal tipped, black
as her dress, hit the wood floor,
rapped at the bars.

I couldn't find my reflection
in the mirror towards the end
as the cane found my back, her
words slapped against it
to make it straight, her hand pressed
at my tender stomach, *suck it in, tighten up;*
keeps you from that old woman's pot belly -
her black stocking legs bending in
as she lifted her skirt - a plie
Like this, she said, as she shoved
her foot at my feet to spread them wider.

This woman,
her photos black and white
outlined the Spring Lake Community
Theatre at shows.
She danced for Russian Royalty; she
is young and tall and smiling there.

At fifteen,
I sat across from her with my parents
as I looked down at my folded hands,
while they discussed me.

At the end,
I found her smile framed in red lipstick -
The smile I saw in those
pictures - *You're a gifted dancer;*
Rethink this, but not for long...

I thought it was over...

At thirty-seven I spent a weekend
with writers,
said goodbyes to new friends,
moved towards my car
when I overhead one voice
lifting a sleeping leg
higher
a cane warm on muscles -

She's sweet, doesn't she look
like a dancer?

White Milk

The book, earmarked for places to revisit,
The gentle crease of the borrowed book,
Guilty of being struck,
Guiltless of highlighting those pages
And when I return,
It's when the waitress forgets her hands
And brings me the real soda, sugary and sweet
I sip but don't oblige and exchange drinks

With one of my children
The one who is wrinkling her
Nose now over
Calorie free bubbles

But for that instance - the sip
I'm back at my Papa Heyniger's where his
New wife brings my sister and me the sinless cold coca
cola
While we sit quietly listening to Wheel of Fortune

The other glass - is my Grandma Redman's
Who questioned,
Then dared our wants
Bringing us our milk straight

Moonrise

The sweet deep breath taken in after
dinner, knowing my father's call is but
an hour away.

Cut grass rich in summer's soup,
the moonrise considers the still
lit sky.

We poke holes in tops of
coffee can lids, breaking into the fine
plastic with pens and stolen kitchen knives.

The fireflies start to blink as the moon
begins her shift, releases the sun
to visit some other side.

We run laughing, easy to catch
the gentle creatures, dancing
in their rites of romance.

Drunk on neon light, we gather
the earthly stars for wonder,
create a Universe within tin cans.

Soon the moon sets with my father's
call and we come running. Our window
to the night then must become dreams.

The morning brings emptiness, the can
left open, most have left this makers'
jail, but some have clung to prod and poke.

ee Blind Mice

Waves of energy push the proa
forward, against the current

of your heart. Winds turned while
you were fishing. I am at the edges of

this lake watching. Bored children
wanting to discover...Laughter and feet,

hands and fury, supper is on the table. I
am where it is shallow, where it is no longer

deep. A field mouse I fed hangs sweetly
on the cat's tongue. A Master over the

lion takes away its toy. Holding it, it is
sweeter on a cupped hand and safe. I see

she releases the pipa on land. Shock and
betrayal, it's a fish out of water.

* *Proa, a type of sailboat*

* *The Surinam toad, or pipa toad (Pipa pipa), is a highly aquatic frog native to northern South America, widely described in the scientific literature because of its remarkable reproductive habits. Surinam toads might be described as "aesthetically challenging."*

Farmhouse

Quiet now…The six children sleep as
ducks in a row - bills buried in the feather

of their blankets. Screams stilled by the
winds of descending hours. Black, the darker

fall of this landscape comes back as memories
developed and overexposed.

There is nothing but the creak of hardwood floor
under my step as I search the narrow hall-

way for the bathroom. In the corner a fly buzzes
closer to my soul than my ear. It is here that I

write poetry under the dim light searching the
mirror for wrinkles that I can't iron, searching for

the deity that stands by my bed side. I'm safe
knowing the daily paper won't come to my door,

though the TV by satellite shouts execution day
nears for Saddam. I am not home - Only the shrills

of waking children will bring me to the roadside
where there will be a cell phone without reception,

where I will comb through the tangle of forest for -
deer. I'm day-dreaming, revisiting my weave in

between the shadows, the trunks of trees all bark
until they peak to sun-light, in between these rows

of fir planted by a hand that meant to sell away.
I'm thinking about the graves of strangers in the

backyard, thinking about the story of the owner so
long ago being a Nazi, thinking about the house here,

right here in the Catskills willed to the Nazi cause,
here in my jeans and t-shirt thinking about the eggnog

my grandma used to pour into Santa mugs on the formica
covered coffee table near her Christmas Tree skeleton-like

and bearing the ornaments I brought as gifts. She lived too
beyond the trees, beyond the distance of where family really

can go. Still we drove there conditioned by duty, conditioned
by guilt, conditioned as the fly banging into walls in winter

crossing thresholds of seasons by a dial. When some Hand turns
to our channel, I hear her, *Thank God for my blue eyes, blond hair.*

Changing the Blade

Daily, I run the tap for my bathwater
adjusting the hot and cold
until it is a temperature I can stand

to shave the stubble that has erupted
from my legs over the night.
Rarely I change the blade

but still catch flesh
as I move over the hills of my body,
the fresh blood emptying itself,

swirling into the clear liquid I sit in.
I think of Jimmy Hendrix, the guitarist,
who could run his fingers along the strings,

combing the Indian, the African, the white
hand holding out of his eruptions,
emptying the cuts into the air

as it swirled into the world he sat in
until he changed the blade,
too fresh, it suffocated

Tenebrae

If the tree is our base in this game of tag
Then why do we run in the summer shorn grass
Shrieking when it gets too close, giving away our friends
Hiding places, distracting the chaser until we can dive at
The roots that cracked open the earth
To this lair we've named our own
Knocking knees and staining them green
Daring It until we are It, until we chase them, those
Others
Who also want to win at this game
Of course, there are no winners
Because when night falls
My father will bellow out our names
In a thunder leaving its echo weaving in and out
Of each hiding place
And though this night we might not have been found
Dusk hurdles itself on us another day
And we circle
With the eldest fist upon fist singing us out and
Keeping us in
Daring the game to chart
Our stars
As the seagull that hungers -
Above me, he's high now
Thinning out the milky way of ocean
Stretching his wings to tip me over sideways
I can see my back clearly now
And hear them now running, laughing, sometimes
Crying

If the tree is safe in this game of tag, then
Why don't we stand still
And climb it like they do in fairy tales
I am singing from my grave
Be Jack, Be Jack
Be very, very still
Don't leave this safe place, but climb it
Until you are above the clouds
But I am remembering now the ax
And that story,
The golden eggs and Lent

In the Roman Catholic tradition, candles are extinguished during the Service of Light during the Easter Vigil Mass on Holy Saturday.

Mint Garden

nothing natural
about our drink of
sweltering days

reflections
on…
back when,

back when my
father
dared to grow
our gardens

patch of mint
leaves
breaking off

from our searching
little
fingers

slips them
into icy, sugary
tea

a mix from that
large tin
scooped out

by
mother's hands
daily

filling our stomachs
and hearts
with summer

All Those Winters Ahead of Us

I wasn't taught by any member
Of my family
How to knit scarves

But I was shown by the cousin
Of a friend how to take those needles
And work them between my

Small fingers
Until the blue ribbon
Chained itself to make a

Sheet- a blanket. I started that
Summer-
The one when the passion of

Creating worked its way through
Me
Like hands moving my heart and

Soul as two long needles.
The scarf I decided was for my father,
For all those winters ahead of us.

Supermarket

I've stepped into the world,
This small
Shopping market in Jersey.

I'm taking rolls
Off the shelf from El Salvador,
Choosing my green plantains

Eyeing up
Mexican flat bread
With a yeast of curiosity

Emptying the last of
Caribbean snap pops
In my basket

At the check out line
Wafer like sweets,
Peanut butter something

And coconut bars
Dyed, red, white, and green
A flag of pride in dessert

Pay the girl who realizes
I can't speak her language,
She hands me my change

That I put
In the bagger's tip container
I step out into the sunshine,

Find my beetle machinery,
Slip behind a wheel to
A destination frozen

In another Time,
But shifting under the shelf
Warm waters already began

To reach,
The tip
Of my southern landscape

I know I'm ready
Because my heart pangs
He chased me down, a glow

Off his young Jamaican skin,
Smiling widely,
Thrusting excitement at me

In a card
A card that said
My friend joined the US Navy

Knowing it was too late,
I could not
Mother my student

So I beamed back,
Good my friend,
And I told him a truth,

My grandfather
Did just what you did,
My Gibraltarian Papa

He had a good life I said, *wanted*
For nothing.

Hour Glass

We watch them make
their way towards
the lifeguard stand

wait from the bench
with a Rent-a-John behind us

a door swings
and we know just where we are -
laughter from the beach
echoes familiar tones
empties itself in our laps

Comfortable chatter rests on
a slice of the orange moon
rests against our horizon

rises in the summer's breeze,
bridges us to the open skies
from our nave

No longer strangers, patience for their
dance on the open beach

the hint of flesh behind the white linen
of his shirt
arrests now from the corner of my eye

widens at each button
A stolen kiss,
a rare moment and he motions me to clear

my vision,
time-keeper, the hour-glass of the ascending moon
becomes this mirror

I'm here because

I could never feel the rush of competition
or the ball in my hand or at my feet

though I'm here now over the ice, listening
for the skates' abrasion on the floor

under their feet. The money spent, the
extra ticket wasted on me who stares

over the exuberance of the crowd. You
see, it's not that I hate the game or am

even disinterested. I just can't be on the
outside of something I would love. I'm

watching the spectators, those who know that
game, maybe they've played it, maybe they

just gave it over to someone else. The slap
of sticks, the puck smacks a windowed wall

and I'm alive with my poetry. I'm in the rink
working those muscles that I push at everyday.

At the moment, I'm thirsting over the well of
a fight, arching my neck over the roar, sinking

into my Western Civilization classes, thinking on
the Romans, sipping at the straw of my Gladiator cup.

Answers

A rhythm bursts
Out and
Into fingers
Wags my
Paintbrush
To the forest

Where the bears walk
And play,
Where the frogs
Are brightly
Exposed -

To the places where
Kangaroos
Jump over the moon
And the sun
Is reachable

To shores
Where the sun
Melts into
Rainbow skies
And surfboards
Wait
For mornings

Where horses
Cling
To seaweed

Still this music
And there is
A cat
Orange and
Staring at me

Chases
Now the blues
And yellows
Of butterflies

Until they leap
From
My brush
To my page

Ass

Child's Game -

I've been spinning blindfolded
aiming my tail
in some direction that entices me
to win a prize

all the time thinking
I'm in line
competing to get the closet

when I've been the donkey
on the wall

Bee Keeper

Apiarist,
He calls me to wear
The veil of poetry, to
Pen my suit

And enter the buzzing,
Swarming hives

And with bare hands,
Move frame by frame,
With the smoker nearby

To steal away and taste
The queen's honey

Waves That Knock You Down

It comes to me, that wave, the one that
yanks you underneath,
where pulls and bubbles grab you deeper in

It comes when I'm thrown against a choice
to value life
or teach it, or release it

when my small son wants to kill outside bugs
not because they are hurting him now,
but because they breed

or when we fish to fish,
and when the fight to live, the struggle grabs harder to a hook
that will not cease to let the trout gulp air

It comes when spiders crawl my walls
and dare me to crush them
and when I throw away bad meat

It's like those waves that knock you down
that you pray so dearly for the ocean's lull,
that blue burp to break her rhythm

so you can gain your strength and swim, swim on.

mon Aban Deng

Scars across his
Forehead- tribal- I know
It's tribal

But I hear his words- his stor-
y
Sudan is under attack- gen-
Ocide and slaver-
y

Still here- still alive-
Still here- here

Where nothing should
Be still
We are the statue- the flag

That calls for right- rite
Of passage
I'm finding his scars above
His brow- line

They aren't there because
Of- no they aren't there to mark
Him by my guide-

Lines- but the lines- the scars- how
I remember
Sudan and my fines- find

Time- find time to sign
A letter
Against a barbarous crime

Despair (For Allen and Debby Murphy)

It is not going anywhere. It has knocked on all
our doors. I am watching her, my friend of

sixteen years. I am watching her march with
Elmo, do diaper runs, sing silly songs, and film

her daughter's tears. They come because Elmo
left and reappeared on a birthday cake. She cried

because what was dear was dessert. Mommy's
magic turns the faucet off with sweet words

singing. It is all this but something more stared
down. I listened to her story, the one to China,

the one where she took a cab with another
called on mommy. There they went, alone

unarmed in language braving the unknown roads,
the roads they traveled, the roads that led to

another birthing place. She called it Nicki's
"finding place." Finding place, it sung somewhere

deep oaring me away from listening. I heard
about the cab driver whose language sounded

angry, but they knew it could not be because
of the laughter that whistled between the lost

rapport. I heard about the return back to the
hotel. I heard how my friend asked the doorman

to show the driver the photo of Nicki. I heard
how he smiled his understanding. I listened still

to the echo, the echo that commanded my
attention. I never really took the ride back with

her. I am still standing in front of them here. I
am standing in front of their finding place.

Finding Time

I'm standing over it
peering into the glass dome

probing its gears with a
curious mind that teeth eat away -
pushed by the rhythm

of one tick

turning away from this mantel
to dress my wrist
in the sweeping motions of the Rolex
I dance with it

forgetting
the feast is still the same

Hold the Word

A voice of slumber awoken
With an affair
Of the soul- that steals away
Time
To only paint and return it

A different color- actor playing
Nurse,
The hidden doctor
With a scalpel of insight removes

The stones- one by one
Piling them in corners
Of my mouth- weighting

My lips
Where I-
Hold my words

Ode to Deceit

Thankless, bottomless, it slithers
Legless
Beneath the seas of
Business, friendship, marriage
Cramping you with a strike-
A bite
That the band plays louder- louder
Still

It attacks me- the apple seed- a core of
Mine- mine that holds me-
My skin, my bones, my muscle-me
My soul-
This me that loves so-
Loves the leaves that color on trees
Loves the colors we wear
The nappy hair-
The bluer eyes born from a hybrid
of heat

How I'm stung-
Stung with a question-
Why trick? Why hide?
If you don't like me-
Don't swallow me up but let me go
Because I'm not a rat-
Not a rat- that runs to squalor
All your cupboards-
All your attics-
All your drawers

No not I- not I
I won't sing to you-
Won't salute you-
Won't wave your flag of colors-
Won't- won't

This is not my song to you-
Deceit
This is my-
My apple rotten to the core

Drowning

From New York to the Jersey Shore
his body traveled
washed up on sands indefinable

Four days later
I read in the daily newspaper
dental records point to an artist's madness;

Lost his girlfriend to suicide,
Left his wallet and note behind
before wading out to lose himself in the sea.

Coastal margins ask me to sail another day
and love the salt that marks me fallen
Come as you are the church preaches

They won't judge me by my clothes
but they have forgotten all hands held up
act in harmony

Had I not danced today for all my woes,
fought the villain one step at a time
I'd be in the throes of Jeremy Blake's travels,

lost and found by fishermen
churning over
and hung in the incessant tree.

My daughter, *Baby Bohemian*
traces paper with poetry, writes
I stand in front of a broken glass looking out

I wonder what it would be like to live in the city
I look at all the buildings
There are lots of things I hope not to see.

Headstones Fall

We're driving through the winding
connected roads where the tombstones
pattern the well-groomed grass like dominoes

In some way I wish
they could be pushed over,
and kept out of my way,

All I can think is why,
why bury ourselves and take up space,
but I can't say this

it rings an unwelcome song in my inner ear
because we are laying flowers at his grave -
It's pop pop's birthday.

The flowers,
they're from the nice Asian lady in the city
The lady I've passed every afternoon

I ask the prices, *5 dolla*
she points to a small bunch near my feet,
6 dolla, 15 dolla; she points above them.

I find a five and a one loose in my hand -
For this I have a white and red rose, a white
carnation and something purple

makes my bouquet happy, like this stand in the city,
like the tomb, the black slab that reads
"No Rain, No Rainbows"

We return to the car.
I hum to myself yes, yes, ok -
ok that is it, *no rain, no rainbows, no rain, no rainbows*

Yes!
and my two children climb into the backseat
and ask how, how people die

All I can say is heart attacks and cancer,
sometimes just old age, like my grandma;
my grandma, her body just got worn

Someplace behind me,
someplace in the rearview mirror of my wake,
the wake where I pushed my headstone,

I watch one by one
as the headstones fall until
I look at the sky and the rainbow.

Paean

a hymn of
snowflakes outside
your window

closer to you and
a million miles
from my desk

and I'm strumming
my air guitar
to their light fall

a paean - blowing towards
many candles
wishes

banging things in
streets
this winter night

waking me from my
bed to
look out kitchen windows

where she questions - laughing
"What am I looking for? - You can't
see Wind."

On the Burner

seasonal
they come with
their cages

that spread across
our
ocean floor

flat and open-doored
tempts
me

with the fishy head
or fleshy tail
and I'm

hungry for the squid
but there is
none today

because I can
see
images of you

and me together
from this murky bay,

while they snap
up their strings
filling buckets for the feast

Wanting to Land

I realize it is morning and I am still waking and
groggy. The kitten's play - roll of my pen over
the hard wood floor laid with the scribble I called
poetry before I turned out the lights last night -
I muse with eyes still closed how I think of her
as kitten -she is not -she is three years old

Perhaps she was the runt or the missing leg
lost so early kept her body small. I connect
with her, youth and size linger on my body
as on hers, people tell me I should be happy.
It's a compliment to be told I look so young.

Still - in my morning dreams between these worlds
I remember how I always loved the air of college -
knew I'd return to teach but I never saw the future -
the day when I would walk the halls or enter
my first classroom, the one where I am
seen as a student, where colleagues ask things like

What chapter are you on in Western Civ.?
and I say philosophy and he says back
Like a woman, that figures- I don't believe in philosophy-
What about strategy and battles? Isn't that the most
important part of history?

And I even think this ancient professor may be right.
And still I think I'm after something else anyway
that I'd like to land where poets do in a field of dandelions
where I imagine the dandelions linger white and transparent

holding words on self-made parachutes
hoping for a strong wind to blow.

Birds at My Window

You see I'm telling him,
the birds don't come anymore
now that you've changed feeders.

But he insists they'll figure it
all out, as if there is a smell
to the seeds laying flat in kitchen foil.

It's been a week now,
only a few sparrows who've
already made their home stop by.

But they're not as bright as the
cardinals dancing, not as charming
as the turtle doves, or not as black

as the starlings or occasional crow.
No they don't seem to know. The
old clear funnel gave their eyes a

feast. At these heights they need
to see. *I want to sit on this deck* he
says *where I'm not near shit and seeds*

and more shit so he isn't, but I am.
I'm near shit and sour seeds. All
I know is I need to yank the chain,

pull it down, but I don't, not yet but
the shit is beginning to stink enough
and I'm thinking about flushing it

all away

Puddling Water

Why should any animal, off on its own,
Choose to give up its life in aide of someone else? - Lewis Thomas

Last night's rain collects into small pools
by the roadside, and I stop my morning walk

to coo over twelve baby ducks
and I call my friend -
I know she will understand my fear
for the small creatures

because cars are racing down this side street
where I stand spotted with mud
She gives her low guttural call
to the ducklings when they near me

I try the same call with my talk, try to guide
them back to the bay but they refuse, take
their own path

Later my friend returns my call and the message
rolls over my heart about a groundhog
beaten over by a parade of blind drivers -
Even calls to police officers aren't answered

Morning after morning I dare myself,
take the same path
where I can't keep myself from counting

they're moving; one, two, three -
one, two, three, four...
five, six....

Ten...

Today, they only reach my fingers

Between Two Pictures

I knew, I knew
was the whisper
of intuition
and my belly
I hold in contemplation
of its hallowed
Eve
and the days
only numbered
you
to an early grave.

There is no face
I can imagine
but my own
and I rock
thoughts of you
on a shelf
between
two pictures.

The corner
I tend
to paint myself
in
is only to ask
why
you left so soon.

Easel

Paper says, man went for a stroll
With his dog;
Stray volt and he loses his best friend

Investigation reveals
A lost street lamp with roots of wires
Never sealed

Here is where I find God,
The primal source of light,
Energy - raw
This fire always glowing;

Attended and its current lights
Dark streets,

Unattended--it kills

Lick the Edges Around the Cone

yes, there is me
but to know only this can be genocide

of cells, of mind and I fight
a winning battle

because
there
is
me

an open shop serves the community
of builders and demolition

grants them the use of my heavy
machinery

And then there is
this poem
of me

from a man who has met my soul
without the skin

nor bones nor muscle
or veins to that beating heart
that quivers to end its
delivery and sell over the business

because I can't
be *me*

from a cage of fashion or wealth
that's rationed

I am not the jaguar
but the cat
small like the kitten

caught playing in notes
of the rustle that a plastic bag makes
and blinded

I grow fearful and

run
run
run

the handles around my neck
tied to my -
frozen in a stampede

from room to room
banging in a dance of madness

until I dive into
the thin space between

the couch and wall

Then there is you
the mindful watchful owner
tearing off the bag when I can
no longer run

freeing me from the play
that bound me

And then there
was this soldier

set to the fields with arms positioned
sent to be more
than *Ikia*

an agent of wills
a storm of action
a torrent of rain
under the desert sun

assigned to bigger names
and pulled in directions

Then there is me
marking classroom boards
with thirsty markers

with thirsty
markers

because the secretary won't give
over the new, capped colors

that will paint the rules
of composition to the door
of this English classroom

Such a poem sweet man
I don't deserve

For I am not a Queen of Kings
or an Artist among Artists

I am nothing
nothing but a kiss *perhaps*
of God in passing

like the snow on a season that
cancels a day of classes

or the DNA
to bones of a declared Jesus

That the world
wants to deny

Marked by Mary

It's a place I need to go after I have been caught
in the rain without umbrellas, without the poncho -

I would like to be the mother who can protect her
children from the storms, the scary thunder, the

roaming volts. There was Hershey Park and then
Great Adventure, a day of clear but marked skies

where the dark descended without warning. We ran
to the car grabbing our small children's hands, trampled

on, trampled the crowds around us. It's that feeling
when clothes are wet, when they are heavy, soggy,

when shoes meet water from the inside. There was also
the day of the horse race, the rains the day before where I

sank into mud knee deep, where shoes emptied were
filled with both earth and earthworms. I hum songs like

Coalminer's Daughter or entertain stories where we go
from *Rags to Riches*. And then there are stranger places

where I take myself to, like my trip to Portugal that
directed me to Fatima , where Mary appeared to small children,

shepherds in a field, tending sheep or when my ex called
me to take a drive to Old Bridge - his church, Polish,

Catholic to celebrate the apparition of Mary on the cactus
cloth - that story, the story of the poor farmer in Mexico

during the Conquest. The yellow bloom of out of season
cacti flowers, the ones rolled up for proof that she indeed had

come. And then her eyes studied so that we saw her as a
living apparition, the eyes that captured the bishops and

priests as the poor farmer opened up his arms. That Mary
and the one that came to me in Jersey , the one I first heard

about in the newspaper - opened press over coffee. I drove
there too, to Passaic to see how God carved her into a tree

stump found by a poor worker, in a poor neighborhood, under
an overpass. I caught her on camera through the lens of

believers who built her an open air temple and adorned her
with gifts. I spoke about her in an essay on poetry, loaned

it to a student and met her again. A book left in a department
mailbox, where I'm taught she's been to Egypt too. I am on

a pilgrimage chased by rains, running to my car, wet with
excitement because I know we are all running there, pushing

by security guards and gates, and still stopping for mothers
pushing their babies in carriages. I am on a pilgrimage

because life has taught me that hot days bring thunderstorms,
that soggy clothes bring discomfort, that early risers still catch

the rides in amusement parks though even then we can't go on
every ride. I went to the Fatima young and as a tourist and

took pictures but didn't listen. I listen now, read the books
Santos left behind. I am on lines to rides I know can kill trusting

the boys to check my safety belt, trusting the builders instinct to
know how to keep all those nails in place, trusting

that I will after the hour get a thrill on the minute ride.

Diet

Lizard lips smack on mealworms
And he comes alive
Not from hunger
But from a wintered diet of crickets

History is this -
A steady diet of the same keeps me thin,
Keeps me ill

History is this -
Eat it to know it and this teacher swallows

Little boy asks, what if?
What if the mealworms fall into the water?
I say, they drown

Ok . . . what if?
What if the mealworms land on wood?
I say, they won't

But I'm not the lizard or any of this
I'm the otter facing the lizard as the tree
And I gnaw away with history

Language

A treat -
We are walking ten blocks to Gee Gee's -
the beach arcade
where quarters are spent
like gamblers slapping down dollars in a sweat
to gain another round

If the token lands just right
amongst the sea of coins
pushed by a metal sweeper they'll cash
in their points for candy

The steps there -
baby birds dead like fallen apples
and I'm explaining a way to mother -
the animals' way

stepping over my words, their's
like the bald fragile bodies before us
remembering March
and how this town is recognized on the map

the sick woman - her boy
the kitchen knife

his small body pushed out a second story
window
the birds and their wings
her sentence and the cell

I feel my pocket where it bulges with one dollar bills
with "deformity" falling from my lips - lingering
fingering

a place determined by language

Red Ribbon

I left that place,
the one where I had
become
the hetaera.
The promises to leave
came to be as the machine
to the heart.
Yet the heart could run
no longer on unwelcomed
sorcery.
So I answered the heavens
to search the market
where the red ribbon
is plenty.
I wear it on my
left wrist.
The silver chain it's twisted in
is stamped, "Italy."
It doesn't matter,
I know it's a reminder
that I can't return
to the delivery
as the goat's stomach.
The red ribbon...are you wondering, it's still there.

* Red string wound around the tomb of the great Matriarch, Rachel,
located in Eretz Israel. In Kabbalah, a protection against the evil eye.

In the Mirror Mother

Hair kept
but tauntingly wild
of an unknown wind.

My mother, I remember
always had delicate feet, feminine
with soles hardened and cracked.

Always, I remember the duality,
painted toenails some sheer pink
bought from the dime store and splattered.

I try to hide these soles.

The lazy cat here has landed on my papers;
he only makes me smile
and I kiss him gently pushing him away.

That too, I inherited…

Hair kept,
but tauntingly wild
of a known wind.

I had laid next to him, the cat, that is
and he reached his paw towards my tied hair
releasing the strands as he pulled away.

One hit, please...

I've come from the pool
and I'm still
in my bathing suit - not the bikini
kind but the halter top, just a little
revealing. I'm hanging onto the
fence like I always
do, watching my son play baseball -
watching my husband
coach. I do it because that is
what wives are suppose
to do here, knowing my suit
is out of place, reveling
a little that it is out of place.
I hear the adults and their
enthusiasm, watch children sit
down in fields, kick dirt,
and throw tantrums, watch every
one yell at the teenage umpire
for making bad calls - bad calls? And
I recall my son
striking out, my son throwing
down his glove, stepping on it - yelling
Damn it! Damn it! Damn it! How
I was the only one
horrified, how they have
yet to win a game - I'm tired and the wind
shifts, goose pimples raise
and offer me another chance
to chat with my mother-in-law

whose jacket hangs
lonesome and leaned
on over the fence. She gives it
up, gives up the stories on Andy, that
he dated so and so and that he
was athletic, that his parents
divorced and that was a shame - she
went to school with his parents
and did you know? -
And Andy became Kim and Kim
became Sue and Sue became
Betty and Betty became...And I think
about oral history,
try to see all
of this in another light because
today I wear her jacket. Maybe
she is a poet, a communion
over a fence, finishing stories in between
rah rah's. And I daydream -
my office mate and her stories,
how she stops me from listening
further, catches me when I take
notes with my mind,
I wanted to vacuum but it was too
late at night, and too early in the
morning, Christine -
My mother-in-law is still talking,
Betty's children are neglectful
and she is happy
that she can't relate. I am
nodding - wishing this poet
would put it on paper. Our attention
back on the game, my son is

up to bat, she is squeezes
my hand and says, *I'd*
sell my soul to the devil,
one hit please...

Cutting Paper

A red velvet sack holds the question
My son pulls a card from the pack
And turns to my father, Pop Pop
Which are you most like...rock, paper or scissors?

He answers: *Rock.*
My son says he is like scissors
Because he goes through things;
My daughter says paper because she is gentle.

There was no *because* after (my father's) rock.
I changed planes while listening:
If my father is rock, am I the pond he skimmed,
Or the simple ripple?

I create hopeful images of Chinese paper cutting
Pretending just maybe
There is in families an art form
When we cut raw material.

Season

A red velvet sack holds the question
My son pulls a card from the pack
And turns to my daughter
What season is your family most like?

They both decide on spring
He says we are not like the heat,
We are just starting the heat;
She says our family isn't rough like winter.

Next question: *When Jesus comes back,*
Where do you think he will go first?

My husband answers Disneyland
I answer Jersey
And realize
We swelter under a summer sun.

Gardner

My seven-year old
daughter
heard her read
poetry at the Clifton
Barnes & Noble. In
the car she said she liked it
because it was about family.

She took a signed book to bed
that I had to ease away
gently. Later,
my husband would ease
the same book away from me,
slide my glasses off -

I opened my eyes, smiled,
and went back
to sleep.

Flood

The sky has given over
its bitterness.
Out of the dark change
all day long
rain falls and falls
as if it would never end. - Williams Carlos Williams, *Spring*
Snow

The Passaic River rises
as the tide of emotions before every family holiday.

This week it's time off and homebound.
My mother's ritual,
her cranking out of hallmark cards,
the ones I toss aside
and can't forgive myself for not opening -
A dare to resurrect
every family friend and member who has
entered our history's halls.

I am at that holiday table, the one with guests
that make your hair stand on end
and the children crawl.

I am eyeing my mother's Easter ham, the one
dish my father uses cloves to stab
in pineapple and wrinkled cherries - The slab
from the can that bakes in a raisin sea.

Yes, the rains of this sort of holiday,
a Nor'easter that found the glory
of Paterson's falls, city parking lots now docks
for Easter plates.

This obstacle - a flood on Paterson's
schools
that throws the teachers
in drums over our Niagara Falls
who swim to graves of remains -
skeletons of industry
that promised once a living god.

All we have in this storm
is the oil
to slick their tongues in language
so I pull the cloves out and pile
the tires of pineapples
in a garage
and tend the ham

with new recipes.

Forever

I asked him if he'd love me after I got old
and my ass got fat and he asked, if you
find a diamond do you throw it
out because it ages a bit?

And I thought about old sayings, that
diamonds are forever

I think they are unless you're my mother
who applauded so hard
after a Johnny Cash concert
that her diamond flew out of the engagement ring

or if you're my sister
who would have it examined
for clarity - or me

The one who accepted diamonds from
man to man to man
only to thrust it back, have it lost,
or sold for money.

Soli Deo glori

For my husband and children with special gratitude to several individuals and groups for their support and insights into the creation of some of these poems: Maria Mazziotti Gillan, Adele Kenny, and the US1 Poets.

Christine Redman-Waldeyer, poet, playwright, and professor, teaches English in Paterson, New Jersey at Passaic County Community College and lives with her husband, daughter, and son in Monmouth County, New Jersey. She earned her doctorate from Drew University, her MA from Monmouth University, and her BA in English from Georgian Court University.

Her creative dissertation, **A Poet's Easter: A Healing of Mind, Body, and Spirit** included in her introduction award winning Caribbean poet, Lorna Goodison and Dr. Tom Worthen, author of **Broken hearts . . .healing: young poets speak out on divorce.**
Prior experience includes teaching full-time in the English Department at Middlesex County College where she was literary advisor of the Arts & Literature Magazine, Myriad, winner of the Columbia Scholastic Silver Crown award 2005. In addition to teaching literature and writing, she has taught history in many colleges and universities in New Jersey, including Seton Hall University, Georgian Court University, Ocean County College, and Brookdale Community College. As a freelance journalist, she has written articles for several newspapers in central New Jersey and co-advises the Passaic County Community College newspaper, *Visions.*

Gloria Rovder Healy, fellow Monmouth County resident and widely recognized New Jersey poet, calls *Frame by Frame* "an exciting collection of poems by poet Christine Redman-Waldeyer. She shares the most intimate moments of her life frame by frame and she does this openly and honestly, often taking the reader off guard. Her poems are both subtle and suggestive urging the reader to read on. The book is a journey of discovery about Christine's life but also a journey of discovery for the reader. I found myself reliving moments with my mother and old boy friends that I thought were buried. *Frame by Frame* is a collection of lyrical poetry telling a frank and honest story and deserves to be in every poet's collection."